The Westward Movement

BY
CINDY BARDEN

COPYRIGHT © 2001 Mark Twain Media, Inc.

ISBN 1-58037-182-5

Printing No. CD-1528

Mark Twain Media, Inc., Publishers
Distributed by Carson-Dellosa Publishing Company, Inc.

Table of Contents

About the American History Series

Welcome to *The Westward Movement,* one of 12 books in the Mark Twain Media, Inc., American History series for students in grades four to seven.

The activity books in this series are designed as stand-alone material for classrooms and home-schoolers or as supplemental material to enhance your history curriculum. Students can be encouraged to use the books as independent study units to improve their understanding of historical events and people.

Each book provides challenging activities that enable students to explore history, geography, and social studies topics. The activities provide research opportunities and promote critical reading, thinking, and writing skills. As students learn about the expansion of the United States and the people who influenced history, they will draw conclusions; write opinions; compare and contrast historical events, people, and places; analyze cause and effect; and improve mapping skills. Students will also have the opportunity to apply what they learn to their own lives through reflection, creative writing, and hands-on activities.

Students can further increase their knowledge and understanding of historical events by using reference sources at the library and on the Internet. Students may need assistance to learn how to use search engines and discover appropriate web sites.

Titles of books for additional reading appropriate to the subject matter at this grade level are included in each book.

Although many of the questions are open-ended, answer keys are included at the back of the book for questions with specific answers.

Share a journey through history with your students as you explore the books in the Mark Twain Media, Inc., American History series:

Discovering and Exploring the Americas
Life in the Colonies
The American Revolution
The Lewis and Clark Expedition
The Westward Movement
The California Gold Rush
The Oregon and Sante Fe Trails
Slavery in the United States
The Civil War
Abraham Lincoln and His Times
The Reconstruction Era
Industrialization in America
The Roaring Twenties and Great Depression
World War II and the Post-War Years
America in the 1960s and 1970s
America in the 1980s and 1990s

Time Line of *The Westward Movement*

1783	The Treaty of Paris established the Mississippi River as the western boundary of the United States.
1789	George Washington became the first U.S. President.
1796	John Adams was elected president.
1800	The U.S. population reached five million.
	Thomas Jefferson was elected president.
1803	The Louisiana Territory was purchased from France for $15 million, nearly doubling the size of the United States.
	Meriwether Lewis and William Clark began a transcontinental expedition.
1804	President Jefferson was reelected.
1805	Lewis and Clark reached the Pacific Ocean.
1806	Zebulon Pike began exploration of the American Southwest.
1807	John Colter explored the Yellowstone area.
1808	James Madison was elected president.
1809	Meriwether Lewis became governor of the Louisiana Territory.
1810	Pacific Fur Company was started by John Jacob Astor.
1812	The War of 1812 between the United States and Great Britain began.
	President Madison was reelected.
1816	James Monroe was elected president.
1818	The border between the United States and Canada was established from Lake of the Woods to the Rocky Mountains.
1819	Florida was purchased from Spain.
1820	President Monroe was reelected.
1821	Mexico won independence from Spain.
1823	Stephen Austin established the first American settlement in Tejas (Texas).
	President James Monroe proclaimed the Monroe Doctrine.
1824	Jim Bridger became the first white man to see the Great Salt Lake.
	John Quincy Adams was elected president.
1826	Jedediah Smith led the first party of Americans overland to California.
1827	Dr. John McLoughlin built the first lumber mill in the Pacific Northwest at Fort Vancouver.
1828	Andrew Jackson was elected president.
1830	Joseph Smith established the Church of Jesus Christ of Latter-day Saints.
	Congress passed the Indian Removal Act.
1832	President Jackson was reelected.
1833	Samuel Colt developed a revolver.
1834	Fort Laramie was established.
1835	Texas war for independence from Mexico began.
1836	Sam Houston was elected president of the Republic of Texas.
1831–1838	The forced Indian removal from the East to Oklahoma occurred. This was later called the "Trail of Tears."

Time Line of *The Westward Movement*

1840	William Henry Harrison was elected president.
1841	John Bidwell organized the Western Emigration Society.
	William Henry Harrison died; John Tyler became president.
1843	Jim Bridger and Louis Vasquez established Fort Bridger.
	The "Great Migration": 1,000 pioneers left Independence, Missouri, on a 2,000-mile journey to the Willamette Valley.
1844	Mormon leader Joseph Smith was killed.
	Brigham Young became the new Mormon leader.
	James K. Polk was elected president.
	The first long distance telegram was sent.
1846	The Oregon Territory became a part of the United States.
	The Mormons were forced to leave Nauvoo, Illinois.
	The Mexican War began.
	The Donner Party met disaster.
1847	The Mormons established Salt Lake City.
1848	James Marshall discovered gold while building a lumber mill for John Sutter.
	Mexico ceded Arizona, California, Nevada, New Mexico, Utah, and western Colorado to the United States in return for $15 million after the Mexican War.
	Zachary Taylor was elected president.
1849	By the end of this year, 80,000 people had arrived in California in search of gold.
1850	President Taylor died; Millard Fillmore became president.
1852	Franklin Pierce was elected president.
1853	The Gadsden Purchase was acquired from Mexico for $10 million.
1856	The first American camel expedition set out from Texas.
	James Buchanan was elected president.
1860	The first Pony Express rider left St. Joseph, Missouri.
	Abraham Lincoln was elected president.
1861	The Civil War began.
	Transcontinental telegraph service began.
1864	President Lincoln was reelected.
1865	The Civil War ended.
	President Lincoln was assassinated; Andrew Johnson became president.
1867	Alaska was purchased from Russia for $7.2 million in gold.
1868	Ulysses S. Grant was elected president.
1869	The Transcontinental Railroad was completed.
	Major John Powell began exploration of the Colorado River.
1872	Yellowstone became the first national park.
	President Grant was reelected.

Name: _____ Date: _____

The Beginning of the Westward Movement

The westward movement across North America began shortly after the first colonies were established. Although most people settled along the coast or in port cities like Boston and New York, a few people were always a bit braver, more adventurous, or more foolish than the rest.

By the time the French and Indian War ended in 1763, people had settled in much of the land as far west as the Appalachian Mountains. King George III tried to prevent further western colonization by issuing the Proclamation of 1763.

1. Use reference sources to learn about the Proclamation of 1763 and why it was issued.

_____

_____

_____

_____

In 1769 Daniel Boone set out with five other men to explore the "western frontier," the area beyond the Allegheny Mountains through the Cumberland Gap. During the next two years, he explored as far west as the present site of Louisville, Kentucky. The Transylvania Company hired Boone in 1769 to lead settlers to Kentucky. His trailblazing efforts established a new route used by thousands in the first major westward migration.

After the Revolutionary War, the Treaty of Paris (1783) set the Mississippi River as the western border of the United States, and "the West" meant all the way to the Mississippi River.

As the population of the original thirteen states grew and the economy developed, the desire to expand increased. For many Americans, land represented potential income, wealth, and freedom. Expansion into the western frontiers offered opportunities for self-advancement.

Each time people moved west and settled an area, "the West" moved farther west until it met the Pacific Ocean.

When he was in his mid-60s, Daniel Boone left Kentucky to settle in Missouri. He claimed he was leaving Kentucky because it was "too crowded."

Name: _____   Date: _____

U.S. Expansion

In 1803, President Thomas Jefferson purchased 831,321 square miles of land from Napoleon, the ruler of France, for $15 million. Known as the Louisiana Purchase, the acquisition of this area nearly doubled the size of the United States, and the movement west gained momentum.

The Spanish were the first to explore and colonize Florida, but by 1815 the area had become a refuge for runaway slaves, buccaneers, and pirates. Many Americans thought Florida was part of the Louisiana Purchase. When settlers poured into the area, Spain objected.

After two invasions in 1814 and 1818 by American troops, Spain decided to sell the area before it was taken by force. In the Treaty of 1819, Spain sold all land east of the Mississippi River and all claims to the Oregon Territory for $5 million. The United States also agreed to give up all claims to the part of Texas acquired in the Louisiana Purchase.

The United States acquired additional land from Great Britain in 1818, which established the border between Canada and the United States from the Lake of the Woods to the Rocky Mountains. This included a small part of South Dakota, parts of northern and western Minnesota and the eastern and northern parts of North Dakota.

Territory north and west of the Louisiana Purchase (present-day Oregon, Washington, Idaho, and parts of Montana, Wyoming, and Canada) were claimed by both the United States and Great Britain. Both had established trading posts and settlements in the area.

Neither Britain nor the United States wanted to go to war over the issue and an agreement was finally reached in 1846. The United States received all land south of the 49th parallel except Vancouver Island.

1. What was the cost of the Louisiana Purchase per square mile?

    _____

Using the map on the next page:

2. Label the states that were formed partly or totally from the Louisiana Purchase.

3. Color Florida green.

4. Label Oregon, Washington, Idaho, Montana, and Wyoming on the map.

Name: _____ Date: _____

The Country Grows

Use the map below to complete the activity on page 5.

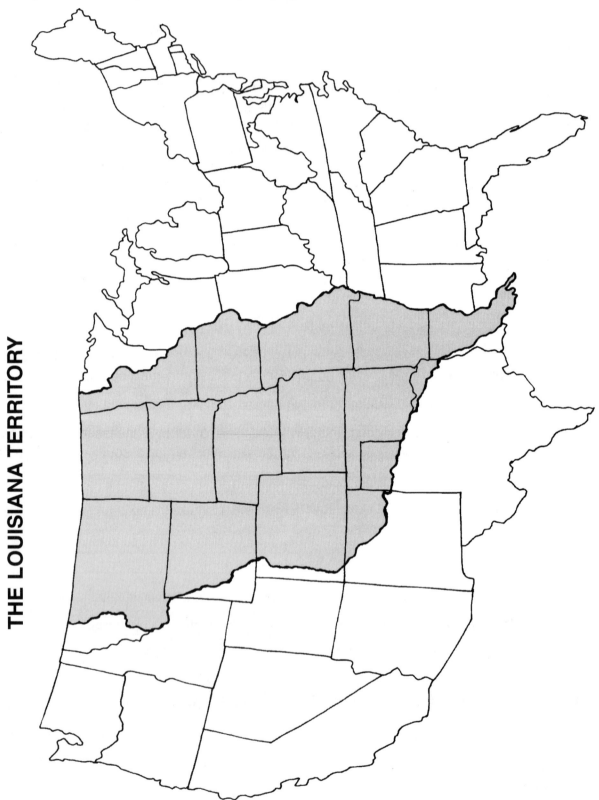

Name: _____ Date: _____

Expanding into the Southwest

After Mexico won independence from Spain, the lands once claimed by Spain became part of Mexico. This included the present states of Texas, California, Nevada, Utah, Arizona, and New Mexico, and parts of Colorado and Oklahoma.

Although the United States had agreed to give up claims to Texas in the Treaty of 1819, thousands of American ranchers, farmers, and adventurers settled in Texas. The Mexican government permitted Americans to establish settlements in their territory, if the settlers agreed to become Mexican citizens.

Disagreements arose between the Mexican government and the Texans. Finally, the Texans ratified their own constitution and declared Texas an independent republic in 1836. After defeating the Mexican general Santa Anna and his troops in the war for independence, Sam Houston was elected president of the new republic.

In 1845, Texas was annexed by the United States, but there was a dispute over exactly where the border of Texas was. War between Mexico and the United States broke out a year later. To end the war, Mexico signed the Treaty of Guadalupe-Hidalgo, giving up claims to Texas and California, most of New Mexico and Arizona, all of Nevada and Utah, and parts of Idaho, Wyoming, and Colorado in exchange for $15 million paid by the United States.

In 1853 James Gadsden negotiated the purchase of land south of the Gila River (southern Arizona and New Mexico) from Mexico for $10 million. This completed the acquisition of land in the continental United States.

If Mexico had not lost the war, much of what is now the southwestern part of the United States would have remained a part of Mexico, making Mexico a far larger, more powerful country.

1. Why do you think the Mexican government was willing to permit settlements in their territory? What would they have gained by having Americans settle in their territory?

    _____

    _____

    _____

2. On the map on the previous page, color the states red that were acquired in the Treaty of Guadalupe-Hidalgo.

3. Using reference sources, color the Gadsden Purchase blue on the map.

4. Look at the areas you colored red and blue. Imagine this as part of Mexico, rather than the United States. What country would you be living in now, Mexico or the United States?

    _____

Name: _____ Date: _____

Manifest Destiny

Once it became an independent nation, the United States experienced a rapid increase in population due to immigration and high birthrate. Since agriculture was the basis for the economic structure of the country, large families to work the farms were an asset. The U.S. population grew from more than five million in 1800, to more than 23 million by mid-century.

This population explosion increased the need to expand into new territory. As parts of the Louisiana Territory became settled, ordinary Americans began walking, riding, and driving wagons over the immense mountains to reach the fertile farmlands of Oregon and California. Some historians estimate that nearly 4,000,000 Americans moved to western territories between 1820 and 1850.

In 1845, a New York editor wrote: "It is America's 'Manifest Destiny' to overspread and to possess the whole of the continent which Providence has given us for the development of the great experiment of Liberty and federated self-government entrusted to us."

Americans believed that Manifest Destiny was both a right and an obligation. However, the rights of Native Americans who claimed the same land were ignored. Those who resisted were either forcibly removed or killed.

Frontier land was usually inexpensive, and sometimes even free, promising a better life for those who didn't own land. Some people moved west simply because they desired adventure. The discovery of gold in California in 1848 and the completion of the Transcontinental Railroad in 1869 were other factors that attracted people to the West.

1. Use a dictionary to define the following words.

   Manifest _____

   _____

   Destiny _____

   _____

2. Explain in your own words what you think the New York editor meant.

   _____

   _____

   _____

   _____

   _____

Name: _____ Date: _____

Expansion Fever Continues

Even after gaining control from the Atlantic to the Pacific, the United States continued to grow. When the Czar of Russia agreed to sell Alaska for $7.2 million, Secretary of State William Seward jumped at the chance to acquire more territory.

Not everyone thought Alaska was a good buy. The purchase was nicknamed "Seward's Folly," by those who believed the purchase of "icebergs and walruses" was a waste of money. In 1959, Alaska became the 49th and largest state.

By 1875, Hawaii had become a regular port of call for American ships in the Pacific. The U.S. had established friendly relations with the island government, and Americans gradually took control of the sugar industry. They also tried to control the government. When the Hawaiian royalty tried to regain control in 1893, Americans living there overthrew the government. They presented a treaty of annexation to the United States. President Cleveland refused the treaty, and the islands became a republic until 1898 when the Hawaiian Islands became a U.S. Territory. Hawaii became the 50th state in 1959.

1. Americans believed it was their Manifest Destiny to control the continent from coast to coast, yet few attempts were made to expand north into Canada or south into Mexico. Why do you think they didn't try harder to expand in those directions?

   _____

   _____

   _____

   _____

2. Using reference sources, learn more about either Alaska or Hawaii. On your own paper, describe the area, who lived there, what countries claimed part or all of the area, and how it eventually came to be part of the United States.

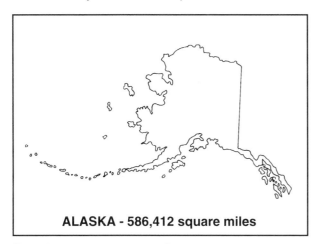

ALASKA - 586,412 square miles

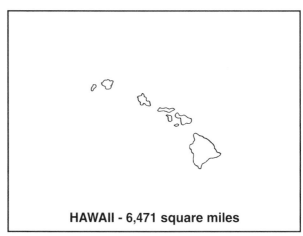

HAWAII - 6,471 square miles

(Drawings are not to scale.)

Name: _____ Date: _____

Native Americans in the East

From the time the first European settlers began colonizing North America, there were conflicts with the Native Americans. What happened to the Narraganset, the Mohican, the Pokanoket, and other once-powerful groups of Native Americans? For two hundred years, the population of those and other tribes dwindled in the East as Whites pushed westward.

One of the few tribes to coexist with the Whites for any length of time were the Cherokee living in northern Georgia. In 1828 when Andrew Jackson was elected president, gold was discovered at Dahlonega, Georgia. Gold fever swept the South, and the Cherokee people were attacked, their lands taken, and treaties broken.

When the Cherokee tried to use the legal system to protect their rights, the governor of Georgia stated, "Treaties were expedients by which ignorant, intractable, and savage people were induced without bloodshed to yield up what civilized peoples had a right to possess."

President Jackson was not sympathetic to Native Americans. When the Supreme Court ordered the federal government to protect the Cherokee nation from attack, Jackson refused to send help. He believed the Indian Removal Plan was the only solution to all conflicts between Whites and Native Americans. This plan involved resettling all Native Americans who lived east of the Mississippi River on land west of the river.

Some members of the Cherokee nation wanted to fight this plan in court. Others wanted to go to war. Some made plans to hide in caves in the hills. Others simply gave up and moved west.

Before the plan became a law, the state of Georgia organized a lottery to give away the Cherokee land to the winners.

1. How would you have felt about the Georgia governor's statement if you had been a Cherokee?

   _____

   _____

   _____

2. What do you think of the Indian Removal Plan? _____

   _____

   _____

3. What would you have recommended the Cherokee do if you had been a Cherokee leader?

   _____

   _____

   _____

Name: _____ Date: _____

The Trail of Tears

Under Andrew Jackson, the Indian Removal Act became law. This affected all Native Americans east of the Mississippi, not only the Cherokee.

In the winter of 1831, the forced removal of the Choctaw began. The government had agreed to feed and clothe the people during their journey, but the money was never spent on provisions for them. Many were barefoot; most had no coats or blankets, yet they were forced to travel on foot across the frozen Mississippi River.

The Creeks were put in chains and forced from their homes in 1836 by U.S. soldiers. About 3,500 died of hunger and exposure before they reached their new territory. The following year, the Chickasaw were also forced to leave.

A long court battle delayed their removal but did not help the Cherokee. In 1838 their nightmare began. An army of 7,000 men dragged the people from their homes without warning and herded them into camps with nothing but the clothes they wore.

An estimated 17,000 Cherokee men, women, and children began their journey to Oklahoma on what came to be called the Trail of Tears. About 25 percent of those who started died along the way. It took nearly six months for those who lived to reach their destination.

Of the five major tribes east of the Mississippi, only the Seminoles tried to fight. After a long, bloody war, they too were defeated and forced to move.

1. Why do you think the journey was later called the Trail of Tears?

    _____

    _____

    _____

    _____

2. Use reference sources to learn more about one of the "Five Civilized Tribes" (Creeks, Cherokees, Choctaws, Chickasaws, and Seminoles). On your own paper, describe where they lived, their lifestyles, their experiences during the forced relocations, and what happened when they arrived at their new homes.

Name: _____ Date: _____

Homes on the Range

When trees were available, settlers built log cabins and wood frame houses. On the plains where there were few trees, earth was the only material available for building, so that's what the settlers used.

Bricks of sod about one foot wide, two feet long, and four inches thick were cut from the prairie. Each brick weighed about 50 pounds; cutting enough bricks of sod was backbreaking work. The long, tough roots of prairie grasses were difficult to hack through. The cut bricks were then stacked, grass side down, to build one-room houses. Boards were laid over the doors and windows to support more bricks. For the roof, the settlers used a frame of poles covered with brush and more sod. The floor was packed-down dirt.

Nicknamed "soddies," these homes provided insulation against heat and cold. They didn't burn easily, like wooden homes. However, the homes were damp and musty most of the time, and they were impossible to keep clean all of the time.

Bits of dirt frequently dropped from the ceiling and walls when it was dry. When it rained, the floor and walls turned to mud. Mice, bugs, and snakes felt more at home in the sod houses than the settlers did, and the settlers weren't too happy about having to share their homes.

Advantages of Log Cabins

_____

_____

_____

_____

Advantages of Sod Homes

_____

_____

_____

_____

Disadvantages of Log Cabins

_____

_____

_____

_____

Disadvantages of Sod Homes

_____

_____

_____

_____

Name: _____ Date: _____

Life on the Prairies

Settlers on the prairies had to contend with extreme heat, bitter cold, droughts, floods, wind, and snow. Lack of trees meant lack of firewood for cooking and heat; instead, dried bison dung was burned.

Water was also in short supply and often had to be carried long distances. In summer, even wells and streams could dry up.

Another big problem with life on the prairie was the isolation. The nearest neighbor might be 10, 20, or more miles away.

One reason people stayed, even under such harsh conditions, was because the Homestead Act of 1862 allowed the head of a household to pay a small filing fee for 160 acres of land. If the family lived on the land and farmed it for five years, it was theirs free.

1. If the government made a similar offer today, do you think people would be willing to accept the offer if it meant building their own homes and living under the same conditions the pioneers did? Why or why not?

   _____

   _____

   _____

   _____

   _____

2. How well do you think you and your family could cope with living conditions like those described in a sod home on the prairie?

   _____

   _____

   _____

   _____

3. List ways the lack of neighbors could increase the problems of living on the prairie.

   _____

   _____

   _____

   _____

Name: _____ Date: _____

Who Were the Mountain Men?

Novels and movies have portrayed mountain men as poor, unsociable, unwashed, and grizzled older men, wearing dirty clothing, and in need of a haircut. They were depicted as men who spent most of their lives hunting and trapping, far from civilization.

Jim Bridger

That image may have been true for a few mountain men in the early 1800s, but they were not all like that. Most mountain men went into the fur trapping and trading business to make money, and for a time, these men could earn large sums of money. Many were young men in their late teens or early twenties who became trappers and hunters for only a few years. Jim Bridger began his long, colorful career as a mountain man at the age of 17.

Mountain men probably didn't bathe often and wore dirty clothes, but few people at that time took baths or changed clothes very often. Did they have long, uncombed hair? They probably did, but so did a lot of other men at that time. Were they unsociable? Some might have been, but not all of them were. Many were married and had families. Many would travel in large groups to a central camp, and then each would set out in a different direction to set traplines.

Most surprising, not all mountain men were men! A few mountain women also made their livings trapping and hunting.

Not only were the mountain men a symbol of America's wild frontier, their role in westward expansion was also very important. They did not simply wander around the Great Plains and Rocky Mountains waiting for people to tell adventure stories and tall tales about their lives. They were explorers and guides who helped settle the land west of the Mississippi.

Select one option.

1. Use reference sources to learn more about one of these mountain men: Kit Carson, Jim Bridger, Jim Beckworth, Jedediah Smith, Thomas Fitzpatrick, Etienne Provost, Hugh Glass. Write a report and include maps and illustrations.

2. Use reference sources and write an essay on the influence of mountain men on the West.

3. Write a tall tale about a mountain man or woman. Include illustrations.

Name: _____ Date: _____

Fur Traders Led the Way

Fur traders in the upper Missouri River area relied on Native Americans to bring bison hides to trading posts. From there the hides were sent downriver to St. Louis. Manuel Lisa ran the Missouri Fur Company from about 1807 to 1820. This ad appeared in the *Missouri Gazette & Public Advertiser* on March 20, 1822.

> TO ENTERPRISING YOUNG MEN: The subscriber wishes to engage ONE HUNDRED MEN, to ascend the River Missouri to its source, here to be employed for one, two, or three years. For particulars, enquire of Major Andrew Henry, near the Lead Mines, in the County of Washington, (who will ascend and command the party) or the subscriber, at St. Louis.
>
> Wm. H. Ashley.

John Jacob Astor

The Rocky Mountain fur trading system was quite different. There beaver was the fur of choice. Beaver hats were the fashion statement of the day in America and Europe. Beaver and other pelts were sold at an annual rendezvous where buyers and trappers met. The furs were taken by wagons to be sold in larger cities.

The first substantial American fur trading venture was the Pacific Fur Company, which was started by John Jacob Astor in 1810. An expedition by Astor overland laid the groundwork for the Oregon Trail by discovering the South Pass through the Rocky Mountains. This route was later one of the major overland routes to the West.

By 1834, there was little demand for beaver and few beavers left to trap. The fickleness of fashion now demanded hats of silk.

After the fur trade died, the mountain men became invaluable guides and scouts for wagon trains, survey teams, and the army. Their skills in living off the land and their knowledge of Native Americans helped bring many pioneers safely across the country.

1. Imagine you are looking for a guide for your wagon train. Write a help wanted ad for the position, and include the qualifications needed.

HELP WANTED

_____

_____

_____

_____

_____

Name: _____ Date: _____

Narcissa and Marcus Whitman

From the time she was 16, Narcissa Prentice wanted to become a missionary to the Native Americans of the West. However, this wasn't allowed because she was a young, single woman.

In 1836, Narcissa met Marcus Whitman, a doctor and preacher, who shared her desire to bring Christianity to the Indians. They married and immediately made plans to move west with Henry and Eliza Spalding, another missionary couple.

Narcissa and Marcus Whitman

The two couples traveled by stagecoach to St. Louis, and then took a steamboat up the Missouri River to Liberty. There they purchased wagons, supplies, horses, mules, and cattle. They were accompanied on their journey west by a group of fur traders. Narcissa and Eliza became the first white women to cross the Rocky Mountains several years before the first wagon train traveled west.

The group ran into trouble from the beginning, both from the weather and the terrain. Little by little, they abandoned their equipment as it broke or wore out.

The Spaldings decided to settle among the Nez Percé in Idaho, and the Whitmans went to live among the Cayuse in the Walla Walla Valley; there they built a mission. Marcus practiced medicine, Narcissa taught school, and they both preached the gospel.

Some critics felt the Whitmans were too rigid in their ways and made little effort to accommodate Cayuse practices and traditions. The Cayuse were not receptive to their sermons.

As more settlers traveled through the area, the Whitmans spent more time assisting settlers than ministering to the Cayuse. The growing number of settlers and the Whitmans' close association with them caused further alienation from the Cayuse.

When members of the Cayuse tribe caught measles from passing emigrants in 1847, more than half died, including most of their children. Convinced the sickness was a plot to kill them all, Chief Tiloukalt led a raid on the mission. The Cayuse killed Marcus, Narcissa, and 12 other settlers, and then they burned down the mission.

Retaliation by the militia nearly wiped out the entire tribe. The remaining members joined nearby tribes, and the Cayuse ceased to exist as an independent people.

1. On your own paper, write about the Whitmans from the Cayuse point of view. Explain how you feel about them and why.

Name: _____ Date: _____

Overland Routes

By the late 1830s, mountain men had explored most of the routes that later became overland wagon trails. In most cases, they followed the Native American trade routes and hunting trails that had been used for centuries. Since no Native American trail led all the way from Missouri to California, the settlers had to find one for themselves.

Beginning in 1840, people started moving west in large numbers. Members of the "Emigrant Societies" helped establish passable overland trails to the West and wrote guidebooks for travelers.

The first wagon train, known as the Bidwell-Bartleson party, included 69 people who left Missouri in the spring of 1841. The group went as far as Soda Springs, Idaho. There they split up; some went to Oregon, while others traveled to California.

Most trails to the West began at Independence or St. Joseph, Missouri, or Council Bluffs, Iowa. There was never one, single trail to California, but rather several major routes, with variations. Those traveling in wagon trains had to take routes that were not the most direct because of several natural obstacles: the canyons of Colorado, the Sierra Nevada Mountains, and the deserts around the Great Salt Lake.

Depending on their final destination, most groups took either the Oregon Trail, the California Trail, or the Santa Fe Trail.

1. Use reference sources to learn more about one of these three major routes to the West. Write a description of the route taken and obstacles people met along the way.

   _____

   _____

   _____

   _____

   _____

   _____

   _____

   _____

2. Make a copy of a U.S. road map. Trace one route taken by the pioneers in black. In another color, trace the roads people can take today from the same starting point to the same destination.

Name: _____ Date: _____

Traveling Overland

What if you lived in the 1860s and your parents decided your family was going to move from Pennsylvania to Oregon? You know the trip will probably take about six months. For the journey you will travel in a large, sturdy wagon with high sides called a Conestoga. Your top speed will be 15 to 20 miles a day.

People traveled in many types of wagons, but the Conestoga was considered the best and was the most expensive. They used horses, mules, or oxen to pull the wagons.

Conestogas were nicknamed "prairie schooners" because their high, white canvas tops looked like sailing ships as they crossed the sea of grass on the American prairie. The strong, broad wheels allowed the wagons to cross rutted roads, muddy flats, and the non-roads of the prairie. The curved floor was designed to reduce load-shifting. Conestogas were capable of loads of up to six tons!

Some of the wagons had a convenience called a "flapp-a-doodle"—a box with shelves for food and cooking utensils—bolted to the rear of the wagons. The back of the box was a hinged door with wooden legs. When the door was lowered, the legs swung down, and the door became a table. The "flapp-a-doodle" was a combination of a kitchen table and a cupboard.

1. If people traveled 20 miles in a ten-hour day, how many miles per hour would that be?

   _____

2. At an average of 15 miles per day, how long would it have taken to travel 100 miles?

   _____

3. Which would take longer: 100 miles in a covered wagon or 1,000 miles in a car going 60 mph?

   _____

4. What were the advantages of a flapp-a-doodle?

   _____

   _____

   _____

Name: _____ Date: _____

Preparing for the Journey

The pioneers couldn't stop for additional supplies along the way. Everything they needed had to be carried with them. The typical covered wagon was four feet across and ten to twelve feet long. Much of that space was filled with food. This is what was needed for one adult to make the six-month journey:

200 lbs. flour	10 lbs. salt	$\frac{1}{2}$ bushel dried beans
10 lbs. rice	5 lbs. coffee	75 lbs. bacon
25 lbs. sugar	2 lbs. baking soda	$\frac{1}{2}$ bushel corn meal
30 lbs. flat, cracker-like bread	1 bushel dried fruit	

Berries or edible roots could be gathered along the way. Hunters sometimes found small game and occasionally shot larger animals, such as bison or deer. When they were desperate, they ate snakes and prairie dogs. For the most part, the pioneers ate biscuits and beans, three times a day, day after day after day!

The pioneers also had to bring everything they needed to start a new home and begin farming when they arrived.

1. List other items the pioneers would have needed.

Clothing for One Person	Tools and Other Farming Supplies	Other Items
_____	_____	_____
_____	_____	_____
_____	_____	_____
_____	_____	_____
_____	_____	_____
_____	_____	_____
_____	_____	_____
_____	_____	_____
_____	_____	_____
_____	_____	_____
_____	_____	_____

Name: _____ Date: _____

Getting From Here to There

Most people who journeyed overland along the Oregon or Santa Fe Trails traveled in wagons. Some rode horses or mules. Some even tried walking all the way pushing a wheelbarrow!

In 1849, Rufus Porter designed a plan to fly pioneers to Oregon using propeller-driven balloons powered by steam engines. About 200 brave pioneers signed up for the trip, but Porter's "airline" never made it off the ground.

Another inventor, "Wind-Wagon" Thomas thought that adding sails to wagons would help speed up travel. His invention was a cross between a wagon and a sailboat. He built a prototype, and it worked well for a short time—until it crashed. He kept trying for years, but he never succeeded.

1. List several advantages and disadvantages to each method of travel for a trip of about 2,000 miles.

	Advantages	**Disadvantages**
Wagon:	_____	_____
	_____	_____
	_____	_____
	_____	_____
Riding horse or mule:	_____	_____
	_____	_____
	_____	_____
	_____	_____
Walking with a wheelbarrow:	_____	_____
	_____	_____
	_____	_____
	_____	_____

2. If you had been offered the choice of traveling west by wagon or balloon, which would you have chosen? Why?

_____

_____

_____

Name: _____ Date: _____

Perils Along the Way

Write the descriptions and answers to the following questions on your own paper.

You are a pioneer heading west. It's early morning on a hot, windy day. The temperature is already over 90 degrees. The wind blows the dust constantly across the prairie, getting inside everything. You're sweaty and dirty. The water barrel is almost empty. You must keep going to reach water before nightfall.

1. Describe your day in as much detail as possible.

You are the captain of a wagon train. There is a terrible storm raging. Thunder shakes the earth and lightning flashes. The wind is strong, and it's difficult for the animals to pull the wagons. The trail has become a muddy swamp. Your wagon train left late, and problems during your journey caused you to lose even more time. People want to stop, but you fear more delays may mean that you will run into terrible blizzards in the mountains.

2. What do you do? Stop or keep going? Explain your decision.

3. Crossing wide or deep rivers with wagons and livestock was dangerous. Use reference sources to find out how pioneers made these crossings.

4. Crossing mountains was another peril the pioneers faced. Going up the mountain could be as difficult and dangerous as going down. Why would going up a mountain be difficult and dangerous?

    Why would going down a mountain be difficult and dangerous?

5. You and your family are caught in a terrible blizzard. The snow is coming down so thickly you can't see more than a few feet ahead. You cannot see any of the other wagons. You may be lost. What should you do?

Name: _____ Date: _____

Interview a Pioneer

You are a reporter for a Sacramento newspaper. Your assignment is to interview and write an article about someone who came west in a covered wagon.

Write twelve questions you might ask that person during an interview.

1. _____

   _____

2. _____

   _____

3. _____

   _____

4. _____

   _____

5. _____

   _____

6. _____

   _____

7. _____

   _____

8. _____

   _____

9. _____

   _____

10. _____

    _____

11. _____

    _____

12. _____

    _____

Name: _____ Date: _____

Journal of a Pioneer

John Bidwell, a member of the first wagon train to head west in 1841, wrote an account of the six-month journey from Missouri.

"The party consisted of sixty-nine, including men, women, and children. We had no cows ... and the lack of milk was a great deprivation to the children. My gun was an old flint-lock rifle, but a good one."

When the group was ready to start, they realized that "... no one knew where to go, even the captain ... We knew only that California lay west, and that was the extent of our knowledge." When their guide joined them, the group set out for Idaho. "For a time, until we reached the Platte River, one day was much like another ... We had to make the road [as we went], frequently digging down steep banks, filling gulches, removing stones, etc."

"One of our men who chanced to be out hunting ... suddenly appeared without mule, gun, or pistol, and lacking most of his clothes, and in great excitement reported that he had been surrounded by thousands of Indians."

The "thousands of Indians" turned out to be a party of about 40 Cheyennes, "who did not intend to hurt the man or take his mule or gun, but that he was so excited when he saw them that they had to disarm him to keep him from shooting them."

"On the Platte River ... we had a taste of a cyclone; first came a terrific shower, followed by a fall of hail to the depth of four inches, some of the stones being as large as turkeys' eggs; and the next day a waterspout–an angry, huge, whirling cloud column ... passed ... behind us. We stopped and braced ourselves against our wagons to keep them from being overturned. Had it struck us it doubtless would have demolished us."

By the time they reached Idaho, one person "had accidentally shot and killed himself ... another had left us at Fort Laramie ... Three [others] turned back ... to return home."

Half of the party continued on to Oregon and the other half to California. "The days were very hot, the nights almost freezing. The first day our little company went only about ten miles ..."

They encountered "thickets so dense as to exclude the sun, and roaring little streams in deep, dark chasms ... paths which looked untrodden except by grizzly bears."

1. On your own paper, make journal entries for three other events that may have occurred while a wagon train traveled west.

Name: _____ Date: _____

The Donner Tragedy

Everyone who traveled west by wagon train faced many hardships and difficulties. Considering the weather, mountains, deserts, lack of water, little food, hostile natives, sickness, and disease, it's a wonder so many actually completed the journey.

One of the most tragic stories was of a group of 87 men, women, and children who left Illinois in a wagon train headed for California in April 1846. For a time, they traveled with a much larger group. They then learned of an untried route recommended in *The Emigrant's Guide to Oregon and California,* which claimed the route would cut 300 miles from the journey. So the group, which was led by George Donner, split off from the larger party to try the new route.

Rather than being a shortcut, the route they chose caused many delays as they hacked a trail through the Wasatch Mountains in Utah and faced an 80-mile stretch of desert. They were harassed by hostile natives who stole their oxen. Arguments among members of the party led to several killings. Some wagons had to be abandoned along the way.

By the time they reached the Sierra Nevada Mountains, it was late in the season. Their supplies were running low. An intense early blizzard forced them to turn back from the attempted crossing.

Some members of the party took shelter in an abandoned cabin, some built crude cabins, and others lived in tents while blizzards raged, day after day. In spite of several attempts to cross the mountains, only one group succeeded, and only seven of the 15 survived to reach Sutter's Fort, a distance of over 100 miles. Rescuers tried many times to return for the rest of the group, but were unsuccessful because of the weather.

When rescue parties finally arrived four months later, those who were still alive were sick and starving. In desperation, some had resorted to cannibalism to survive. Of the original party, only 47 lived to see California.

One survivor, Virginia Reed, later wrote about the terrible winter they had spent waiting for rescue. "The misery endured during those four months at Donner Lake would fill pages and make the coldest heart ache."

1. If you had been with this group, would you have wanted to take an unknown "shortcut" or stay on the known routes? Why?

_____

_____

_____

_____

Name: _____ Date: _____

Traveling by Sea

Not everyone who traveled to California and Oregon went overland. Some chose to make the trip by ship.

People living on or near the east coast could book passage on a clipper ship headed for California. The trip around Cape Horn was long, dangerous, and very expensive. Strong currents, icebergs, and fierce winds off Cape Horn caused ships to go off course, adding more time to the journey. The supply of ships did not nearly meet the demand for travel, and many older ships, which weren't very safe, were brought into service.

A second option was to sail across the Gulf of Mexico to Panama. From there, travelers walked or rode horses 100 miles through dense jungles to Panama City in the hopes of catching a ship heading north on the Pacific side. This route was also uncertain, long, and dangerous. Yellow fever, malaria, dysentery, and cholera killed many who attempted this route.

Water Routes to California

New York to Cape Horn	15,000 miles—6-8 months
New York to Nicaragua	5,500 miles—5 weeks
New York to Panama	6,000 miles—6 weeks
New Orleans to Nicaragua	4,500 miles—4 weeks
New Orleans to Panama	5,000 miles—5 weeks

Using the map at the left:

1. In red, trace the route ships took from New York, around South America, to California.

2. In blue, trace the route a person would take from New Orleans to Panama and across Panama to California.

3. Which route would you have taken: overland in a covered wagon, by ship around Cape Horn, or by ship to Panama? Write your answer on your own paper, and explain why you selected that method of travel.

Name: _____ Date: _____

In Search of Religious Freedom

Although the U.S. Constitution guarantees freedom of religion, members of the Church of Jesus Christ of Latter-day Saints, commonly called Mormons, were repeatedly denied that freedom.

The history of the Mormons began in New York. Joseph Smith, the founder of the group, said that an angel had told him where to find a book written on thin gold plates by the prophet Mormon. He translated the writings which became *The Book of Mormon*, the basis for the new religion.

Joseph Smith

As membership in the church grew, nonmembers became very hostile to Smith and his followers. The Mormons moved from western New York to Ohio, to Missouri, and then to Illinois in an attempt to be allowed to practice their religion in peace. Each time they established a settlement, they gained new converts; however, they also gained new enemies and were violently expelled by angry neighbors.

In Illinois, the Mormons founded the city of Nauvoo and began building a great temple. They also began practicing polygamy, which Smith said was God's will.

Public outrage against polygamy was only one reason why Mormons were persecuted. People resented the Mormons' tendency to patronize only businesses owned by other Mormons. When Mormons voted, they all tended to vote for the same person. They also began a system of communal ownership of property that allowed church leaders to redistribute property to those in need.

When Smith announced he was running for president in 1844, he and his brother were arrested and murdered. His followers were threatened: if they stayed, they, too, would be killed.

1. Using a dictionary, define *polygamy.* _____

   _____

2. Use reference sources to learn about the revelations Joseph Smith wrote about in *The Book of Mormon.*

   _____

   _____

   _____

   _____

Name: _____ Date: _____

The Mormons Move West

Brigham Young

After Joseph Smith was killed, Brigham Young, one of Smith's 12 apostles, became the new Mormon leader. Young decided the Mormons would move to the area around the Great Salt Lake because there were no other settlers nearby. He began plans for the move by instructing people to grow extra crops, to store food, and to build wagons.

In February 1846, the Mormons began leaving Nauvoo. By May, thousands were spread out across hundreds of miles of prairie. Those who went ahead set up camps and planted crops for those who followed. They spent the first winter near what is now Omaha, Nebraska. Many died that winter, but the survivors did not give up.

In the spring, Young led an advance party of 25 wagons to the valley of the Great Salt Lake. Two days after they arrived, men began planting crops to ensure there would be food for the others when they arrived. Young returned to join the main group and to lead them to their new home.

Besides being a strong religious leader, Brigham Young also had great organizational skills, which were essential in coordinating the move of thousands of people from Illinois to Utah. He also made arrangements for temporary quarters in Missouri for other converts from the United States and England who would later join them in Utah.

1. List five problems Brigham Young had to deal with when thousands of Mormons left Illinois to travel west.

   _____

   _____

   _____

   _____

   _____

2. Young and other leaders planned the layout for Salt Lake City, which grew to a population of over 12,000 in four years. List five important things that would have needed to have been done to turn a barren stretch of land into a large city.

   _____

   _____

   _____

   _____

   _____

Name: _____ Date: _____

The End of the Trail

After nearly six months of traveling, most wagon trains reached their destinations. Even those who had not met disasters along the way must have been worn out from the trip. But the hard work did not end when the journey was over. Most people who traveled to Oregon settled in the Willamette River Valley where winters were much milder than they had been in the East. This allowed them to plant winter wheat.

For people arriving in Oregon, the first task was to make a claim for land. Congress passed a bill in 1841 allowing each male settler to claim 640 acres of land; an additional 160 acres could be claimed for a wife and each child.

Many of the first homes people built were one-room log cabins, because trees were plentiful. With help from neighbors, a log cabin could be erected fairly quickly. People ate, slept, cooked, and lived in homes that were quite small by today's standards. After living in a covered wagon for six months, however, any home, even a small one, must have seemed like a luxury.

1. How would you have felt once you finally reached your destination?

    _____

    _____

2. Why would the government offer people free land?

    _____

    _____

    _____

3. Before building a log cabin, a site needed to be chosen and prepared. If you were going to build a log cabin, what type of site would you choose?

    _____

    _____

4. What tools would you need to clear the underbrush from an area, cut down trees, and build a log cabin?

    _____

    _____

    _____

5. What materials besides trees would you need to complete a log cabin?

    _____

    _____

    _____

Name: _____ Date: _____

The Pony Express

As more people moved west, the need for quicker communication became more pressing. News could be carried by ship or stagecoach from the east coast to California, but even the fastest methods took nearly a month—much too long for businessmen.

The solution: use the existing stagecoach stops and add more to establish a system of stations every 10 to 20 miles where riders could change horses quickly. Every 75 to 100 miles, fresh riders took over for exhausted ones. By traveling day and night, riders covered the 2,000-mile trip between St. Joseph, Missouri, and Sacramento, California, in ten days.

The first ad for Pony Express riders was placed in March 1860. A month later, the first rider left St. Joseph, Missouri.

WANTED

Young, skinny, wiry fellows not over 20. Must be expert riders willing to risk death daily. Orphans preferred. Wages: $25 a week.

This ad was answered by many young men, including Bill Cody, age 14. The youngest rider, Bronco Charlie Miller, began his career at the age of 11 when a riderless horse with a mail pouch arrived in Sacramento. He took the mail on to the next station, was hired, and continued as a Pony Express rider for five months.

Eventually, the Pony Express had over 100 stations, 80 riders, and 400 to 500 horses. Although the route was extremely dangerous, only one mail delivery was lost during the time the Pony Express was in operation.

Pony Express riders brought news of Abraham Lincoln's election in 1860 and the beginning of the Civil War in 1861 to California. Financially, it was a failure, even though it cost $5 to send mail by Pony Express. The Pony Express closed in October 1861 when the Pacific Telegraph Company completed a line to San Francisco.

1. What other qualities or skills besides those listed do you think a Pony Express rider needed?

   _____

   _____

   _____

2. Would you have wanted to apply for this job? Why or why not? _____

   _____

   _____

Name: _____ Date: _____

What Would They Have Said?

Work with a partner. Take turns writing a dialogue that might have taken place between two Pony Express riders who met at a station during their travels.

Westward Rider: _____

_____

Eastward Rider: _____

_____

Westward Rider: _____

_____

Eastward Rider: _____

_____

Westward Rider: _____

_____

Eastward Rider: _____

_____

Westward Rider: _____

_____

Eastward Rider: _____

_____

Westward Rider: _____

_____

Eastward Rider: _____

_____

Westward Rider: _____

_____

Eastward Rider: _____

_____

Name: _____ Date: _____

The Transcontinental Telegraph

Samuel Morse

The telegraph, invented by Samuel Morse, used electricity to send messages over wires strung on poles. He sent his first long distance message in 1844 from Washington, D.C., to Baltimore, Maryland.

Telegraph operators sent messages using a system called Morse code. Each letter of the alphabet was represented by a different combination of dots (short pulses) and dashes (longer pulses). The person who received the messages translated the code and wrote out the letters and words.

By 1860, most cities on the east coast were connected by telegraph. Slowly the lines were extended westward.

The Western Union Telegraph Company received a government contract to connect telegraph lines from Missouri to Salt Lake City, where another line was already connected to San Francisco.

Thousands of wooden poles were needed to carry the wires across a 1,000-mile area with few trees. About 100 freight wagons carried the poles, the wire, the workers, and the supplies needed to dig the holes, erect the poles, and string the wires.

Once the project was finally completed, keeping the telegraph working became a full-time job for a large crew of workers called linemen. Sometimes wires were deliberately cut. Wind and heavy snow could snap wires. Lightning frequently hit the wires.

One menace to the telegraph lines came from an unexpected source. Bison discovered that telegraph poles were great back scratchers! As the great shaggy animals took turns rubbing against the poles, their heavy sideways movements knocked the poles over. Adding long metal spikes to discourage them only provided more efficient back scratchers.

People who sent telegrams paid by the word, so they used as few words as possible. Rewrite these two messages in eight words or less.

1. Dear Mom and Dad, Your first grandchild, a healthy baby boy, was born yesterday at 5 P.M. We named him Adam Jesse James Winthrop. He has red hair just like Grandpa Joe and eyes like Grandma Eleanor. Alice is tired, but well. Love, your son, Jim.

_____

2. We are planning to visit you in June or July. We will leave from St. Joe around mid-May and take the stagecoach all the way to Sacramento, which will take about a month or so. We are looking forward to seeing you soon. Your cousins, Emma and Fred.

_____

Name: _____ Date: _____

Morse Code

A	•−	H	••••	O	−−−	U	••−
B	−•••	I	••	P	•−−•	V	•••−
C	−•−•	J	•−−−	Q	−−•−	W	•−−
D	−••	K	−•−	R	•−•	X	−••−
E	•	L	•−••	S	•••	Y	−•−−
F	••−•	M	−−	T	−	Z	−−••
G	−−•	N	−•				

1. Use Morse code to decipher this message.

− •••• •   − • •−•• • −−• •−• •− •−−• •••• •−− •− •••

− − − − − − − − − − − −

•− −−• •−• • • −   •• −• ••• • −• − •• −−− −•

− − − − − − − − − − − −

2. Write your own message in Morse code and have a partner translate it. Use the code for one letter above each blank. Skip a blank between words.

— — — — — — — — — — — — — — — — — —

— — — — — — — — — — — — — — — — — —

— — — — — — — — — — — — — — — — — —

— — — — — — — — — — — — — — — — — —

— — — — — — — — — — — — — — — — — —

Name: _____ Date: _____

Traveling By Stagecoach

Have you ever wondered what would it have been like to ride a stagecoach? Between 1850 and 1900, stagecoaches carried tens of thousands of passengers on regularly scheduled routes across the west. Compared to modern transportation, a stagecoach trip was painfully uncomfortable and dreadfully slow.

A newspaper printed this advice to passengers in 1877: "Don't imagine for a moment you are going on a picnic; expect annoyance, discomfort and some hardships. If you are disappointed, thank heaven."

Passengers traveling long distances carried weapons, blankets, water, and food with them. They rode day and night, averaging five to ten miles an hour. One reporter wrote: "The jolting will be found disagreeable at first, but a few nights without sleep obviate that difficulty."

Relay stations every 10 to 25 miles provided rest stops. One passenger reported that at stagecoach stops "the available food would curdle a goat's stomach."

Most passengers rode on wooden benches inside the stagecoach. Mail, baggage, and sometimes passengers rode on seats outside or on the roof. When the stagecoach came to a steep hill, mud, or soft sand, passengers had to get out and walk to lighten the load. The trip from Missouri to California took about a month.

Stagecoaches were not heated or cooled. A blind covered the window, but didn't completely block snow, rain, wind, and dust. Coaches designed to hold nine passengers might actually carry from 15 to 20 people. As coaches climbed hills or made turns, all the passengers could be thrown from one side of the coach to the other.

Overloaded stagecoaches had a tendency to overturn. Passengers faced other dangers, including runaway horses and attacks by robbers.

1. Which method of transportation would you have preferred, wagon train or stagecoach? Why?

   _____

   _____

   _____

   _____

   _____

Name: _____ Date: _____

The Transcontinental Railroad Connects the Country

During the 1840s and 1850s, railroads had become a major means of transportation along the east coast. People and goods could travel more quickly and comfortably by railroad than by any other means available.

The dream of a railroad stretching from one coast to the other became a possibility when the Pacific Railway Bill was passed in 1862; however, the project was delayed until 1865 because of the Civil War.

The Union Pacific Railroad began laying track in Omaha, Nebraska, heading west. At the same time, the Central Pacific Railroad started laying track in Sacramento, California, heading east. To complete the project, the federal government granted the two railroads loans of nearly $65 million and ownership of approximately 24 million acres of land.

The project involved laying about 1,700 miles of track across prairies, deserts, mountains, and valleys. Most of the workers were immigrants. The Central Pacific imported 10,000 Chinese laborers. The Union Pacific hired mostly Irish immigrants.

Building the transcontinental railroad was not an easy task. Workers needed food, supplies, and shelter. Working conditions were dangerous. The weather caused problems and delays. Native Americans resented the encroachment of the "iron horse" on their lands and tried to prevent the railroad from being completed.

On May 10, 1869, the two railroads met at Promontory Point, Utah, where representatives of both railroads drove a golden spike into the final rails. Once the railroad was completed, it was possible to travel from coast to coast in a week!

1. Use reference sources to learn more about how the transcontinental railroad was built. List three problems workers faced and what was done to solve them.

_____

_____

_____

_____

_____

Name: _____ Date: _____

Ways to Travel

Compare these three methods of transportation. Write advantages and disadvantages for each. Use reference sources if you need more information.

	Advantages	**Disadvantages**

Covered Wagon

Railroad

Stagecoach

Name: _____ Date: _____

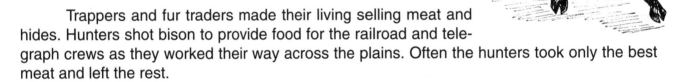

From Herds of Millions to Near Extinction

When the pioneers traveled west, they encountered vast herds of bison. Between 30 million and 200 million bison once roamed the American plains. Although pioneers called them buffalo, the correct word is bison.

Native Americans hunted bison for thousands of years, killing only what they needed and using every part of the animal for food, clothing, and tools. This hunting had little effect on the huge herds.

Travelers who crossed the Great Plains in the early 1800s often heard the rumbling of what sounded like thunder in the distance, even when the skies were clear. Suddenly, the ground began to shake as a huge herd of bison thundered past. Those early settlers and the ones who followed were responsible for the near extinction of the bison.

Trappers and fur traders made their living selling meat and hides. Hunters shot bison to provide food for the railroad and telegraph crews as they worked their way across the plains. Often the hunters took only the best meat and left the rest.

Later, train companies offered tourists the chance to shoot bison from the windows of their coaches. The animals they killed were left to rot in the sun.

People even held bison-killing contests to see who could kill the most animals in the shortest amount of time. Buffalo Bill Cody reportedly shot more than 4,000 bison in two years.

By 1880 bison were nearly extinct. Where millions of animals had once roamed, only a few thousand remained, and even that number continued to decline until only a few hundred remained. People today are working to rebuild the herds of bison that once dominated the Great Plains of the United States.

1. What do you think of killing animals for sport? _____

_____

_____

2. Why do you think it is important to save animal species like the bison from extinction?

_____

_____

_____

Name: _____ Date: _____

Native Americans in the West

Hundreds of groups of Native Americans lived in U.S. territories west of the Mississippi River from the Canadian border to Mexico and west to the Pacific coast. Many had very distinctive lifestyles and cultures. Eventual domination by white society was the only thing they all had in common.

1. Use reference sources to learn about the history of one tribe, its culture, types of homes, economic system, social system, and eventual contact with white settlers. Write a report that includes maps and illustrations.

NATIVE AMERICAN TRIBAL REGIONS

PLAINS				**PACIFIC**
Blackfoot	Halchidhoma	Asatsagewi	Cupeno	**NORTHWEST**
Gros Ventre	Yuma	Yana	Diegueno	Skagit
Hidatsa	Cocopa	Washoe	Kamia	Quileute
Crow	Pima	Nomlaki	Akwa'ala	Quinault
Mandan	Navajo	Yahi	Nakipa	Humptulips
Yanktonai Sioux	Zuni	Western Shoshone	Kiliwa	Chehalis
Aikara	Yavapai	Yuki	Cochimi	Skokomish
Shoshone	Maricopa	Maidu	Ignacieno	Chimakurn
Cheyenne	Aravaipa Apache	Pomo	Waicura	Duwamish
Teton Sioux	Jicarilla Apache	Konkow	Pericu	Snogualmie
Ponca	Coyotera Apache	Gosiute		Puyallup
Yankton Sioux	Hopi	Ute	**PLATEAU**	Coast Salis
Omaha	Papago	Paiute	Sanpoil	Chinook
Pawnee	Tiwa	Wappo	Chelan	Clatsop
Oto	Tewa	Miwok	Columbia	Clatskanie
Arapaho	Towa	Kawaiisu	Kootenay	Tillamook
Kansa	Keres	Patwin	Coleville	Siletz
Missouri	Mimbreno	Mono	Pend d'Oreille	Yaquina
Kiowa		Panamint	Coeur d'Alene	Siuslaw
Osage	**CALIFORNIA/**	Costano	Flathead	Coos
Quapaw	**INTERMOUNTAIN**	Yokut	Nez Percé	Umpqua
Comanche	Northern Paiute	Chemehuevi	Cayuse	Tututni
Wichita	Tolowa	Esselen	Spokane	Chastacosta
Kichai	Karok	Tubatulabal	Walla Walla	Makah
Tawakoni	Yurok	Salina	Umatilla	Coulitz
Tonkawa	Shasta	Kitanemuk	Klickitat	
Lipan Apache	Wiyot	Serrano	Yakama	
	Achomaui	Chumash	Wishram	
	Wintun	Fernandeno	Tenino	
SOUTHWEST	Hupa	Gabrielino	Molala	
Havasupai	Bannock	Juaneno	Wanapam	
Huzlapai	Northern Shoshone	Cahuilla	Klamath	
Mojave	Chimariko	Luiseno	Modoc	

Name: _____ Date: _____

Tidbits of Western Trivia

- In 1842, Francisco Lopez discovered gold dust in the roots of an onion he dug up near Los Angeles. His discovery sparked a local gold rush, but news of his discovery was ignored elsewhere.

- Gold was discovered in Colorado in 1858. As news spread, people rushed to Colorado to get rich. Denver, Golden, Boulder, and Colorado City began as gold mining towns.

- During its 19 months of operation, Pony Express riders covered 650,000 miles and carried 34,753 pieces of mail.

- The youngest Pony Express rider, Bronco Charlie Miller, lived to the age of 105. When the Korean War began, he tried to enlist, but was turned down. He was 92 years old at the time.

- In 1861, Mark Twain wrote, "When crushed, sagebrush emits an odor which isn't exactly magnolia and equally isn't polecat (skunk)—but is a sort of compromise between the two."

- Buffalo Bill Cody had little formal education. When he wrote his autobiography, his publisher complained about Cody's punctuation. Cody replied, "Life is too short to make big letters where small ones will do; and as for punctuation, if my readers don't know enough to take their breath without those little marks, they'll have to lose it, that's all."

- "Home on the Range," written in 1873, was President Franklin D. Roosevelt's favorite song.

- In honor of President Grant's visit to Central City, Colorado, the sidewalk in front of a new hotel was paved with silver.

- The view from the 14,110 foot high Pike's Peak in 1893 inspired Katharine Lee Bates to write a poem that became the song, "America, the Beautiful."

F.D. Roosevelt

- A silver nugget weighing about 1,840 pounds was discovered in Aspen, Colorado, in 1894.

- 700-year-old dried beans found at Mesa Verde were preserved by the dry weather. When planted, they grew. In 1983 two men from Colorado started Adobe Milling, a company that sells Anasazi beans.

1. Use reference sources to find two other tidbits of Western trivia.

_____

_____

_____

_____

Name: _____ Date: _____

The Grand-Daddy of All Canyons

Native Americans knew about the Grand Canyon for thousands of years before Europeans arrived in North America. The first European to report seeing the Grand Canyon was Garcia Lopez de Cardenas, one of the men sent to explore ahead of the Coronado expedition.

Although it is the largest canyon, the Grand Canyon is only one of hundreds of steep canyons along the Colorado River that presented major obstacles for settlers heading west.

The Colorado River has slowly been forming the largest canyon on Earth. Marine fossils embedded in the limestone walls show that a deep sea once covered this area many years ago.

The Grand Canyon is over 200 miles long, about ten miles across, and one mile deep. Four buildings the height of the Empire State Building stacked on top of one another wouldn't reach from the bottom to the top of the Grand Canyon.

From the North Rim to the canyon floor is a journey from pine forests to desert. Deer, elk, bighorn sheep, squirrels, rabbits, porcupines, cougars, bears, and many other mammals, birds, reptiles, amphibians, insects, and fish make their homes in the Grand Canyon.

Visitors come from all over the world to visit the Grand Canyon. Naturalist John Muir called it the "Grandest of God's terrestrial cities."

1. Imagine being an early explorer and seeing the Grand Canyon for the first time. Use descriptive adjectives to write about what you see, hear, smell, feel, and taste as you stand on the edge looking down.

_____

_____

_____

_____

_____

_____

_____

_____

2. On your own paper, write a fictional story about the day you looked outside and found a hole the size of the Grand Canyon in your backyard.

Name: _____   Date: _____

Gold Fever Spurs the Westward Movement

Gold fever began in California in 1848 and quickly spread east across the United States. People in South America, Canada, Europe, and Asia caught the infection. People in every social class and occupation caught the fever by listening to or reading tales of fabulous gold strikes. It affected rich men and poor ones, merchants, farmers, doctors, teachers, and lawyers.

Once infected, the only way to cure the fever was to travel to the California gold mines. Tens of thousands of people swarmed to northern California. Fortune seekers walked, rode horses, traveled in wagons, or sailed thousands of miles in search of a dream.

For most, that dream turned into a nightmare of hardship, disease, poverty, and sometimes death. For every prospector who found enough gold to become wealthy, thousands more lost everything they had and left the gold fields poorer than when they arrived.

Most who traveled to California in search of gold never intended to stay. They planned to make their fortunes and return home, but it rarely happened that way. Whether they found gold or not, thousands made California their home.

1. Describe how you think your life would change if you discovered gold.

_____

_____

_____

_____

_____

_____

_____

_____

_____

_____

_____

_____

_____

_____

_____

40

Name: _____ Date: _____

Wild Bill or Buffalo Bill?

Two famous Bills in the Old West were Buffalo Bill Cody and Wild Bill Hickok. One started a Wild West Show. The other became a U.S. Marshal. But which was which?

Use reference sources to find the answers. Write CODY, HICKOK, or BOTH on the line before each statement.

_____   1.   He was a Pony Express rider.

_____   2.   He was shot and killed while playing poker in Deadwood, South Dakota.

_____   3.   He nicknamed his horse Brigham, after the Mormon leader.

_____   4.   He traveled to Europe with his Wild West Show.

_____   5.   He was born in Illinois in 1837.

_____   6.   He was born on a farm in Iowa in 1846.

_____   7.   Novelist Ned Buntline made him a hero in many exaggerated tales of his exploits.

_____   8.   He joined the Union Army during the Civil War.

_____   9.   He worked as a scout and stagecoach driver on the Santa Fe and Oregon Trails.

_____   10. He became U.S. Marshal of Hays City and Abilene, Kansas.

_____   11. Sitting Bull and Annie Oakley were two of his friends.

_____   12. He worked as a stagecoach driver and a hunter for the railroad.

Wild Bill Hickok

Buffalo Bill Cody

Name: _____ Date: _____

From Rags ... to Riches ... to Rags

Horace Tabor

Born in Vermont in 1830, Horace Tabor worked as a stonecutter until moving to Kansas in 1855. After several unsuccessful years of farming, he and his wife Augusta headed west to join in the Pike's Peak gold rush.

Although Horace Tabor knew nothing about mining, he staked a claim and began mining. To support the family, Augusta opened a kitchen and bakery for hungry miners. When Horace failed to find gold, they moved again. Horace staked another claim; Augusta resumed her food business.

Horace opened a general store and was elected mayor and postmaster, but found no gold. Again they moved, this time to Leadville where silver had been discovered. Augusta continued her business, and Horace opened another store and decided to give up mining. Instead, he provided grubstakes to miners in return for a one-third share in whatever they found.

1. Use a dictionary. What is a grubstake? _____

   _____

2. If you had been a miner without any money, tools, or food, would you have taken up Horace's offer? Why or why not?

   _____

   _____

   _____

   _____

The Tabors' luck turned when Horace made a $17 investment in supplies for George Hook and August Rische. They hit one of the richest lodes of silver ever found! Horace and Augusta received one-third of the profit. They went from poverty to prosperity.

Horace spent large amounts of money, gambled, and made investments in real estate, railroads, and other ventures. They moved to Denver where they lived extravagantly, yet the money continued to roll in. In spite of all their wealth, Augusta was unhappy with their new lifestyle, so Horace divorced her. At the age of 51, he married 19-year-old Elizabeth Doe.

A series of bad investments and the depression of 1893 caused the couple to end up as poor as when Horace had first arrived in Colorado. Friends got him a job as postmaster in Denver because he needed the money. Horace died in destitution in 1899. Elizabeth froze to death in a shack near one of their worthless mines in 1935.

In the West, a person's fortune could change quickly from extreme poverty to immense wealth—or from great wealth to poverty—as the story of Horace Tabor proves.

Name: _____ Date: _____

Camels in the West?

Camels have been used for thousands of years in the deserts of Africa and Asia for transportation and beasts of burden. They can travel long distances with little water, live on tough vegetation that most other animals won't eat, carry heavy loads, and endure both extremely high and extremely low temperatures. They are even able to swim across rivers.

As commander of the first pack train to transport gold from California to the East, Edward Beale wondered if there might be a better way to carry supplies across the desert. Later, while exploring Death Valley with Kit Carson, Beale remembered reading about travelers in Asia who rode camels instead of horses.

Beale's idea was approved by Secretary of War Jefferson Davis. Men were sent to Turkey to purchase camels and hire drivers who knew how to handle them. Beale was in charge of the first American camel expedition in Texas in 1856, which was successful and proved to many people that camels were the ideal pack animal. They could carry twice as much as a mule and weren't bothered by snow, sand, heat, or high altitudes.

Camels were used to transport supplies to mining camps in Nevada, Montana, and the Pacific Northwest. The reign of the camel in the West came to an end a few years later, however, when the transcontinental railroad was completed. Cargo could be carried more quickly and cheaply by trains.

For a time, a few bands of wild camels continued to live in the deserts, and the people who spotted them often wondered if they had been out in the sun too long.

1. What if camels had become popular in the Southwest instead of horses, and cowboys rode camels? Draw a four panel cartoon about a cowboy and his faithful camel, Clyde.

Name: _____ Date: _____

Adventures on the Colorado River

On May 24, 1869, Major John Powell and a crew of nine began a journey to explore the length of the Colorado River. They loaded enough supplies for ten months on their four boats and set off from Green River Station in Wyoming and down the Green River.

The men reached the first canyon three days later and named it "Flaming Gorge," for its brilliant orange and red rocks. Here they found fossils of ancient marine animals who had lived in the oceans that had once covered the western part of North America.

When they reached steep waterfalls or rapids, the men tied ropes to the boats and stood on both sides of the shore to lower them over the waterfalls. Then they carried their supplies down steep, rocky trails to the bottom. At some points, they even had to carry their boats.

Early in June, a boat carrying three men went over a waterfall. The men were saved, but about 2,000 pounds of supplies were lost. A fire at their campsite on June 16 destroyed more of their supplies. At times, the men became discouraged because of the hard work, mosquitoes, and heat.

After almost two months of travel covering 538 miles, the group reached the Colorado River. Although one member left the group, the others continued their journey through beautiful canyons and around cataracts, rapids, and waterfalls. On August 10, they reached the Grand Canyon. By then, their clothes and shoes were falling apart, and they had only a month's worth of supplies left. They also knew that more dangers lay ahead.

When they came to the most dangerous rapids they had encountered so far, three of the men decided not to continue and headed back on foot.

With only two boats and no supplies, the remaining six men finally reached a Mormon settlement on the Virgin River. There they ended their 100-day adventure.

1. Use reference sources to find the names of Powell's four boats.

   _____

   _____

2. Would you have continued the journey to the end or turned back? Why?

   _____

   _____

3. Powell became Commissioner of Indian Affairs in 1873 and Director of the Irrigation Survey in 1888. Use reference sources to find out more about John Powell's achievements.

44

Name: _____ Date: _____

Pecos Bill

The tall-tale cowboy superhero known as Pecos Bill didn't make his appearance until long after the West was won. He first appeared in "Century Magazine" in 1923.

According to stories, he was the biggest, meanest, toughest man who ever rode a horse. Raised by a pack of coyotes, Bill looked for cowboys so tough they could kick fire out of flint with their bare toes.

He swung a rattlesnake for a lariat and rode bareback on a mountain lion. Pecos Bill taught broncos how to buck, and there wasn't anything he couldn't ride. Once he even lassoed a tornado and rode it into town. Pecos Bill feared nothing, but a city slicker was his downfall. When he saw the city slicker decked out in cowboy clothes, he plumb laughed himself to death.

1. Make up a name for a western superhero or heroine. Write a tall tale about that person's adventures. Add an illustration to your story. Use your own paper if you need more room.

_____

_____

_____

_____

_____

_____

_____

_____

_____

_____

_____

_____

_____

_____

Name: _____ Date: _____

Women in the West

During the long cross-country journey west, women faced as many hardships and did as much hard work as men. Many families who began the journey by wagon train, lost husbands and fathers along the journey due to illness, accidents, or hostile Native Americans. When they finally arrived at their destination, the women had to support themselves and their families.

Many women, even though married, supported their families while their husbands started farming, mining, or attempting other occupations. They had invested everything in supplies for the journey and arrived with almost nothing.

At first, even women who were forced to work were expected to follow only traditional occupations like nursing, teaching, cooking, laundering, sewing, waitressing, and working as servants. But many western women soon earned their livings in less traditional ways.

Some opened their own businesses or ran family businesses when their husbands died or left to seek their fortunes in the gold fields. Women became reporters, printers, artists, photographers, doctors, and even hunters, trappers, and miners.

1. Why do you think women were able to break out of traditional roles more easily in the West than they had in the East?

_____

_____

_____

_____

_____

_____

_____

_____

Henrietta Chamberlain King took over the running of her husband's ranch after he died. He left her a half-million acres of land and a half-million-dollar debt. When she died, the estate was worth $5.4 million and included over a million acres of land.

Jessie Ann Benton, daughter of Senator Thomas Hart Benton, married John Charles Frémont, who was assigned to map the Dakota country for the army. She helped her husband plan his expeditions, but the army would not let her travel with him. When he returned, Jessie rewrote the accounts of his trips into interesting reports that were later published as a book. Almost every pioneer heading west carried a copy along on their journey.

Name: _____ Date: _____

Women Gain Rights in the West

Although the fight for women's rights began in the East, the first real gains occurred in the West. In 1861, Kansas became the first state to allow women to vote in school elections and to hold property in their own names. Women were eligible to vote and run for office in city elections in 1887.

In Wyoming, women had the right to vote by 1869 and could serve on juries. By 1914, women had the right to vote in eleven states—all of them in the West.

Esther Morris

Susanna Medora Salter

Nellie Tayloe Ross

Esther Morris was the first woman appointed as Justice of the Peace in the United States. On the day she was sworn in, her husband, a saloon keeper, objected and made a scene. His wife promptly fined him for contempt of court. When he refused to pay his fine, she sent him to jail.

Susanna Medora Salter became the first woman elected as mayor of a U.S. city (Angonia, Kansas) in 1887.

The first woman governor of a state, Nellie Tayloe Ross, was elected in Wyoming in 1925. She later became the first woman director of the U.S. Mint.

1. Susan B. Anthony believed women were allowed to vote in the West because it was easier to write new laws granting equal rights than to change existing laws. Do you agree or disagree? Give two reasons.

   _____

   _____

   _____

2. In what state did Esther Morris live? _____

Name: _____   Date: _____

Who Was Calamity Jane?

There was a woman nicknamed Calamity Jane, but many of the stories told about her exaggerated the truth or were completely fictional. Be a history detective. Use reference sources to search for the truth about Calamity Jane. Write FACT or FICTION on the line before each statement.

Calamity Jane

_____ 1. One of Calamity Jane's jobs was as a bullwhacker—a driver of oxen-pulled wagons used to deliver supplies.

_____ 2. Calamity Jane became best known as the heroine of dime novels written by Ned Wheeler.

_____ 3. Calamity Jane served as a scout for General Custer.

_____ 4. When her family traveled west with a wagon train in 1865, Calamity Jane wore trousers borrowed from one of the men and spent much of her time hunting with the men.

_____ 5. Orphaned at 16, Calamity Jane pretended to be a boy so she could get exciting jobs.

_____ 6. Calamity Jane's skill as a nurse caused many to call her the frontier's Florence Nightingale.

_____ 7. Calamity Jane singlehandedly saved the Deadwood stage from bandits.

_____ 8. Born Martha Jane Cannary, Calamity Jane lived in Missouri until she was 13.

_____ 9. Calamity Jane claimed to have been married to about a dozen different men, including Wild Bill Hickok.

_____ 10. Calamity Jane got her nickname after saving an army captain when he was shot.

_____ 11. Calamity Jane was frequently thrown in jail because she drank too much.

_____ 12. Her autobiography, *Life and Adventures of Calamity Jane*, was a huge best seller that earned her large sums of money.

Name: _____ Date: _____

Colter's Hell

Imagine a place where steam rises from the ground; mud boils, burps, and bubbles; and huge geysers shoot up in the air! When John Colter and other early explorers told of steam rising from the earth, pools of boiling water and mud, hot springs and geysers that spouted fountains of hot water, people thought they were making up stories. The place was nicknamed "Colter's Hell."

Colter's Hell became Yellowstone National Park in 1872, "dedicated and set apart as a public park or pleasuring ground for the benefit and enjoyment of the people." It was named because of the rhyolite, a yellow rock found there. The park covers 3,472 square miles, mostly in Wyoming.

The best-known geyser, Old Faithful, "blows its top" every 40 to 100 minutes, shooting water 100 to 184 feet in the air for about four minutes.

Yellowstone includes more than 10,000 thermal sites. Use reference sources to describe each of these features and how they were formed.

1. hot spring _____

_____

_____

_____

2. geyser _____

_____

_____

_____

3. mud pot _____

_____

_____

_____

4. fumarole _____

_____

_____

_____

5. Myths are stories used to explain something in nature. On your own paper, make up a myth to explain why "Old Faithful" erupts.

Name: _____   Date: _____

Word Search: Enjoy the Wildlife at Yellowstone National Park

Look for and circle the following words in the grid to find the names of 51 types of animals that make their homes in Yellowstone National Park. The words may be printed up, down, across, backward, forward, or diagonally. In all, the park is home to more than 300 species!

BADGER	BAT	BEAR	BEAVER	BISON	BOBCAT
CHIPMUNK	COYOTE	CRANE	CROW	DEER	DUCK
EAGLE	ELK	FALCON	FISH	FOX	FROG
GOOSE	GROUSE	GULL	HARE	HAWK	LARK
LYNX	MARMOT	MINK	MOLE	MOOSE	ORIOLE
OSPREY	OTTER	OWL	PELICAN	PORCUPINE	PUMA
RABBIT	ROBIN	SKUNK	SHEEP	SNAKE	SWAN
TERN	TOAD	TURKEY	TURTLE	VOLE	WEASEL
WOLF	WOLVERINE	WREN			

```
B I M R P K H K W A H G M I F O G I R A B B I T
Z X O Y M K E G U L L B R E T T O T V V H N G Q
F I L D W S R N E C F L X S B R W H O Y K L Q Y
M H E B O J A O T M B T O E A L C X L I P S G B
N E A O A C E S O H S I I R T Z P S E Y E S F O
R A M T L N B I Y E S O O G E V Z U T R L W Y B
V K U R C U E B O L K D S B L G J T E M I O D C
Y O P F I D P L C M C K E S P A D N L W C L S A
V P K F F T S I K W N A Y O R G I A M J A F Z T
Y E C N V P J U C I V K J I S P U A B W N H W Y
K R Y N U P D F M E E P B W U A R P N K R Q K E
I A M I E M Y E R P S O A C N M F R T H C C X K
X H M O C R P G G S I N R Y O Y E O V T O U A R
V O W Q T E W I L Y V O C T L T Z S X Z M U D U
S P D O M S O N H M P W W W R U S K U N K E I T
Z N D R J U V T I C V W O X N E M U K E K A N S
W M D I Q O P U C P O X E L A X Z E A U R X B Z
P L A O M R N R T V E N Q G V J N K D F F V G E
K J X L N G I T U J O Y L D F E A J T P I W N A
W F Z E W Q B L C C O E S L A M R N H H S E T J
F K J L O W O E L R Z A T H D O U I R A H A H D
E R N Y R M R A P V A E Q V E B T V N N K S U G
J A D N C N F R O G V N Q M G E L A I E I E L U
W L R X I T T Q S E J B E S W I P Q C M A L C X
```

50

Name: _____ Date: _____

Music of the Old West

The music of the Old West is a history in melody of those who lived, worked, and died there. Pioneers sang as they trudged across the plains; men sang as they built the Transcontinental Railroad; cowboys sang as they rode the range.

"Across the Wide Missouri" expressed the sadness many felt about leaving their homes in the East, even as they looked forward to a new life in the West. As thousands traveled west, many died along the way. "Bury Me Not on the Lone Prairie" is a grim song expressing fear and loneliness.

A lively song with silly words, "Old Dan Tucker," was often played at square dances.
> "Old Dan Tucker was a fine old man,
> Washed his face in a frying pan.
> He combed his hair with a wagon wheel.
> Died with a toothache in his heel."

The California and Colorado gold rushes inspired many songs, like "The Days of '49" and "My Darling Clementine," published in 1863.

Cowboys riding the range sang songs like "Git Along, Little Doggies," "Night-Herding Song," or "Cowboy Lullaby" to calm a restless herd—or to keep themselves awake on night-long vigils. The best-known cowboy song, "Home on the Range," was originally a poem called "Western Home," written by Brewster Higley, an Ohio doctor. The music was written by Daniel Kelley from Rhode Island. There was one difference between the original song published in 1893 and the one we know today. The chorus, "Home, home, on the range, where the deer and the antelope play ..." wasn't part of the song. Those words were added later by Texas cowboys.

1. Find the words to one of the songs discussed above or listed below. Read the chorus and several verses. In your own words and on your own paper, describe the mood and "story" of the song.

"Ho! Westward Ho!"	"The Buffalo Hunters"	"Sweet Betsy From Pike"
"The Texas Rangers"	"The Yellow Rose of Texas"	"Cowboy Jack"
"The Cowboy"	"The Old Chisholm Trail"	"The Big Corral"
"The Strawberry Roan"	"The Colorado Trail"	"Down in the Valley"
"Cotton-Eyed Joe"	"The Cowboy's Lament"	"Jack O' Diamonds"
"Buffalo Gals"	"The Wabash Cannonball"	"Good-bye, Old Paint"

Name: _____   Date: _____

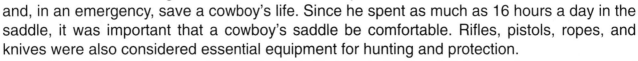

Ride 'em, Cowboy!

Stories of the cowboys of the American West have long been popular in novels, movies, and on television. Most cowboys are pictured as white men, brave and self-reliant individuals.

Cowboys came to the West from all over the world. Many were Southerners, and some from the Northeast. Some were Mexican, some European and Asian. About one in seven was African-American; in Canada, cowboys were as common as in the United States.

Their work was difficult and often monotonous, and they were usually poorly paid. The era of the cowboy matched the years of the great cattle boom (1866 to 1887), when huge herds of cattle were driven along trails to market.

Two of the most important items a cowboy owned were his horse and saddle. A good horse could make his job easier and, in an emergency, save a cowboy's life. Since he spent as much as 16 hours a day in the saddle, it was important that a cowboy's saddle be comfortable. Rifles, pistols, ropes, and knives were also considered essential equipment for hunting and protection.

From their red long underwear to their Stetson hats, the clothing cowboys wore served many useful, practical purposes.

Use reference sources to learn more about the clothing and equipment cowboys used every day.

1. Why did cowboy hats have wide brims? What useful purposes did the cowboy's hat serve?

    _____

    _____

2. What are chaps? Why did cowboys wear them? _____

    _____

    _____

3. Why did cowboys wear high leather boots? _____

    _____

4. What is a lariat? What was it used for? _____

    _____

    _____

5. What are spurs? Why did cowboys wear them? _____

    _____

Name: _____ Date: _____

The Mystery of Mesa Verde

As people settled in the West, they came across many wonderful places, both natural and man-made. One unusual site was discovered on a high flat-topped mountain in Colorado called Mesa Verde.

While searching for stray cattle in December 1888, two men discovered a magnificent ancient city built under an overhanging cliff. They named it Cliff Palace. There they found open plazas and stone houses two and three stories high. Rooms were also dug into the ground like basements. There were no stairs. The people had used ropes and ladders to get from one level to another.

The only way to reach Cliff Palace from the outside was to climb down the side of the cliff using ropes, ladders, and shallow holes cut into the rocks.

The people who built and lived in Cliff Palace left no written records. The dwellings have been deserted for nearly 700 years. The Navajo told stories of "the ancient ones," known as the Anasazi, who once lived in this area.

Archaeologists found many treasures at Cliff Palace, including black-on-white pottery, woven blankets, stone and bone tools, clothing, and bows and arrows. By studying the ruins, they know the Anasazi grew corn, beans, and squash; they hunted deer and rabbits and raised dogs and turkeys. By excavating burial sites, scientists discovered that the people had been short and stocky with black, or sometimes brown, hair.

To protect the treasures found at Mesa Verde, the area was made a national park in 1906.

1. Use reference sources. Who were the two men who discovered Mesa Verde?

    _____

    _____

2. List two advantages and two disadvantages of having no stairs and using ropes and ladders to get from one level to another.

    _____

    _____

3. What would be the advantage of making it so difficult to enter Cliff Palace?

    _____

    _____

4. Would you like to visit Mesa Verde? Why or why not?

    _____

    _____

Name: _____ Date: _____

True or False?

Circle "T" for true or "F" for false.

1. T F   Calamity Jane was a fictional character.

2. T F   John Powell and a group of men explored the length of the Colorado River in 1869.

3. T F   Yellowstone was the first national park in the United States.

4. T F   Horace Tabor died a very wealthy man.

5. T F   The Transcontinental Railroad was completed with tracks laid by the Central Pacific and Union Pacific Railroads and joined near the Grand Canyon.

6. T F   France sold the Louisiana Territory to the United States for $15 million.

7. T F   Two states, Louisiana and Arkansas, were formed from the land in the Louisiana Purchase.

8. T F   Texas was an independent country before it joined the Union.

9. T F   Manifest Destiny was a term used by people who wanted to give equal rights to Native Americans.

10. T F   On the prairies, many homes were made of sod.

11. T F   Alexander Graham Bell invented the telegraph.

12. T F   Most people enjoyed traveling several hundred miles by stagecoach.

13. List three reasons why people wanted to move west.

_____

_____

_____

_____

_____

_____

_____

Name: _____   Date: _____

Fact or Opinion?

A **fact** is a statement that can be verified as true.
Fact: The Pony Express began in 1860.

An **opinion** is a statement that cannot be verified as true.
Opinion: All Pony Express riders were very brave.

Write "F" for fact or "O" for opinion on the line by each statement.

_____ 1. Yellowstone National Park is very beautiful.

_____ 2. Calamity Jane was a remarkable woman.

_____ 3. The Mormons settled in Salt Lake City, Utah.

_____ 4. Tens of thousands of settlers traveled west by wagon train.

_____ 5. Millions of bison once roamed the plains of America.

_____ 6. Polygamy is wrong.

_____ 7. Tall tales about western superheroes like Pecos Bill are fun to hear.

_____ 8. Many Americans believed it was the Manifest Destiny of the United States to control all land from the Atlantic to the Pacific.

_____ 9. Buffalo Bill Cody killed thousands of bison.

_____ 10. The Transcontinental Railroad made travel to and from California quicker and easier.

11. Write two facts about the West. _____

_____

_____

_____

12. Write two opinions about the West. _____

_____

_____

_____

Name: _____   Date: _____

Which Came First?

Using reference sources and the time line on pages 2 and 3, place a check mark next to the event in each group that came first.

1. _____ Joseph Smith established the Church of Jesus Christ of Latter-day Saints.
   _____ Sam Houston was elected president of Texas.

2. _____ War of 1812 began.
   _____ The United States purchased Florida from Spain.

3. _____ Louisiana Purchase
   _____ Treaty of Paris

4. _____ Trail of Tears
   _____ Mexico won independence from Spain.

5. _____ Congress passed the Indian Removal Act.
   _____ The United States purchased Alaska from Russia.

6. _____ Gold was discovered in California.
   _____ The Transcontinental Railroad was completed.

7. _____ The Pony Express began.
   _____ The Donner Party met disaster.

8. _____ The transcontinental telegraph was completed.
   _____ Yellowstone became the first national park.

9. _____ Brigham Young led the Mormons to Utah.
   _____ John Bidwell organized the Western Emigration Society.

10. _____ James Polk was elected president.
    _____ Abraham Lincoln was elected president.

11. _____ The Civil War began.
    _____ Abraham Lincoln was assassinated.

12. _____ Andrew Jackson was elected president.
    _____ The Oregon Territory became a part of the United States.

13. From what country did the United States gain Arizona, California, Nevada, New Mexico, and Utah? _____

14. Who established Fort Bridger? _____

15. Who became president when William Henry Harrison died in office? _____

Name: _____ Date: _____

Westward Words

Define these words. Use a dictionary if you need help.

1. calamity _____
   _____

2. canyon _____
   _____

3. Conestoga wagon _____
   _____

4. Continental Divide _____
   _____

5. "iron horse" _____
   _____

6. emigration _____
   _____

7. frontier _____
   _____

8. gorge _____
   _____

9. immigration _____
   _____

10. tall tale _____
    _____

11. mesa _____
    _____

12. prairie _____
    _____

13. stagecoach _____
    _____

14. telegraph _____
    _____

15. transcontinental _____
    _____

Name: _____ Date: _____

In the News

A newspaper headline is a summary of the most important point in an article. Headlines must be brief, to the point, and grab the reader's attention.

Write headlines in six words or less for each event.

1. The first packet of mail from St. Joseph, Missouri, to Sacramento, California, arrives in ten days by Pony Express.

   _____

2. On May 10, 1869, representatives of the Union Pacific and Central Pacific Railroads drive in a golden spike at Promontory Point, Utah, to celebrate the completion of the Transcontinental Railroad.

   _____

3. While searching for stray cattle, Richard Wetherill and Charlie Mason discover an ancient deserted city, which they name Cliff Palace.

   _____

4. John Colter reports visiting a place where steam rises from the ground and shoots water and steam into the air.

   _____

5. Women in Kansas are allowed to vote and run for office in city elections.

   _____

6. John Powell and five men explore the length of the Colorado River.

   _____

7. Thomas Jefferson arranges payment of $15 million for the Louisiana Purchase.

   _____

8. Secretary of State Seward agrees to purchase Alaska from Russia for $7.2 million.

   _____

Western Heroes and Heroines

Learn more about a person who was important during the westward expansion of the United States. Use the Internet and other reference sources to write a three- to five-page report about one of these people. Add illustrations and maps if possible.

Eliza Spaulding

John Ashley
Moses Austin
Edward Beale
John Bidwell
Daniel Boone
Jim Bridger
Kit Carson
George Catlin
William Clark
Buffalo Bill Cody
Samuel Colt
Davy Crockett
Mike Fink
John C. Frémont
Wild Bill Hickok
Sam Houston
Henrietta Chamberlain King
Meriwether Lewis
Major Stephen Long
James Marshall
Joe Meek
Annie Oakley
Zebulon Pike
Jedediah Smith
Eliza Spaulding
Henry Spaulding
General Zachary Taylor
Louis Vasquez
Marcus Whitman
Narcissa Whitman
Brigham Young

Annie Oakley

Kit Carson

John Frémont

Suggested Reading

The Pony Express by Peter Anderson

Songs of the Wild West by Alan Axelrod

Frontier Home by Raymond Bial

Full Steam Ahead: The Race to Build a Transcontinental Railroad by Rhoda Blumberg

Westward Ho!: An Activity Guide to the Wild West by Laurie Carlson

Settling the American West by James L. Collins

The Black Cowboys by Gina De Angelis

Calamity Jane: Her Life and Her Legend by Doris Faber

The Story of Women Who Shaped the West by Mary Virginia Fox

Children of the West by Russel Freedman

In Search of the Grand Canyon by Mary Ann Fraser

Wagon Train by Bobbie Kalman

Wild West Days by David C. King

Pony Express! by Steven Kroll

How Would You Survive in the American West? by Jacqueline Marley

Buffalo Gals: Women of the Old West by Brandon Marie Miller

West by Covered Wagon: Retracing the Pioneer Trails by Dorothy Hinshaw Patent

Black Heroes of the Wild West by Ruth Pelz

Buffalo Bill by Nancy Robinson

Brigham Young: Pioneer and Mormon Leader by William R. Sanford and Carl R. Green

Welcome to Kirsten's World: 1854 by Susan Sinnott

The Transcontinental Railroad in American History by R. Conrad Stein

The Story of the Trail of Tears by R. Conrad Stein

The Pioneers Go West by George Rippey Stewart

Answer Keys

The Beginning of the Westward Movement (page 4)

1. The Proclamation of 1763 forbade any settlement west of the Appalachian Mountains. This was done because England feared Native American uprisings and didn't want to maintain a large army in that area to protect settlers.

U.S. Expansion (page 5)

1. The cost was about $18.04 per square mile.
2. LA, AR, MO, IA, MN, TX, OK, KS, NE, SD, ND, MT, WY, CO, NM (Source maps may vary.) Teacher check map.

Manifest Destiny (page 8)

1. Manifest: apparent to the senses or to the mind; obvious; clear
   Destiny: the seemingly inevitable or necessary succession of events

Traveling Overland (page 18)

1. two miles per hour
2. 6.66 days
3. 100 miles in a wagon

Traveling by Sea (page 25)

Teacher check map.

In Search of Religious Freedom (page 26)

1. The state or practice of having two or more spouses at the same time; plural marriage

Morse Code (page 32)

1. The telegraph was a great invention.

Wild Bill or Buffalo Bill? (page 41)

1. Both
2. Hickok
3. Cody
4. Cody
5. Hickok
6. Cody
7. Cody
8. Both
9. Hickok
10. Hickok
11. Cody
12. Cody

From Rags ... to Riches ... to Rags (page 42)

1. Money or supplies advanced to a prospector in return for a share in any findings

Adventures on the Colorado River (page 44)

1. Powell's boats were named *Emma Dean*, *Kitty Clyde's Sister*, *No Name*, and *Maid of the Canyon*.

Women Gain Rights in the West (page 47)

2. Wyoming

Who was Calamity Jane? (page 48)

1. Fact
2. Fact
3. Fiction
4. Fact
5. Fact
6. Fact
7. Fiction
8. Fact
9. Fiction
10. Fiction
11. Fact
12. Fiction

Colter's Hell (page 49)

1. A hot spring is a spring whose water temperature is above 98.6°F (37°C). The water is heated underground by pockets of molten rock (magma) and rises to the surface through cracks.
2. A geyser is a spring from which columns of boiling water and steam gush into the air at intervals. The water is in a long, narrow tube. Water at the base of the tube gets superheated and forces the cooler water above it out of the tube by a jet of steam.
3. A mud pot is a bubbling pool of mud. Water from hot springs mixes with dirt and rock particles to form mud.
4. A fumarole is a vent in a volcanic area, from which smoke and gases arise. When pressure builds up below the surface, smoke and gases are forced out of cracks in the surface.

Word Search: Enjoy the Wildlife at Yellowstone National Park (page 50)

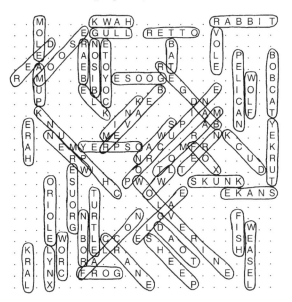

Ride 'em Cowboy! (page 52)

1. The wide brim kept the sun and rain off the cowboy's head and neck. A cowboy could use a hat to herd cattle, carry water or feed, swat flies, as a storage place, and so on.
2. Chaps were pieces of leather strapped on over ordinary trousers. Chaps protected the cowboy's legs from thorny brush, cow horns, and other hazards.
3. Boots were tall to avoid getting the feet caught in the stirrups and to protect the feet and legs from brush and snakes.
4. A lariat is a long rope with a loop on one end used for catching and tying horses, cows, etc.
5. A spur is a pointed device, usually metal, worn on the heel of the rider's boot. It is used to urge a horse forward.

The Mystery of Mesa Verde (page 53)

1. Richard Wetherill and Charlie Mason discovered Cliff Palace.

True or False? (page 54)

1. F	7. F
2. T	8. T
3. T	9. F
4. F	10. T
5. F	11. F
6. T	12. F

Fact or Opinion? (page 55)

1. O	6. O
2. O	7. O
3. F	8. F
4. F	9. F
5. F	10. F

Which Came First? (page 56)

1. Joseph Smith established the Church of Jesus Christ of Latter-day Saints.
2. War of 1812 began.
3. Treaty of Paris
4. Mexico won independence from Spain.
5. Congress passed the Indian Removal Act.
6. Gold was discovered in California.
7. The Donner Party met disaster.
8. The transcontinental telegraph was completed.
9. John Bidwell organized the Western Emigration Society.
10. James Polk was elected president.
11. The Civil War began.
12. Andrew Jackson was elected president.
13. Mexico
14. Jim Bridger and Louis Vasquez
15. John Tyler

Westward Words (page 57)

1. Deep trouble or misery; disaster
2. A long, narrow valley between high cliffs, often with a stream flowing through it
3. A broad-wheeled covered wagon used for hauling freight in colonial America, named for the Conestoga Valley in Pennsylvania where the wagons were made
4. Ridge of the Rocky Mountains forming a North American watershed that separates rivers flowing in an easterly direction from those flowing in a westerly direction
5. A nickname for a locomotive
6. The act of leaving one country or region to settle in another
7. The developing, often still uncivilized or lawless, region of a country
8. A deep, narrow pass between steep heights
9. The act of coming into a new country, region, or environment, especially in order to settle there
10. An exaggerated story of a legendary person or event
11. A small, high plateau or flat tableland with steep sides, especially in the southwestern United States
12. A large area of level or slightly rolling grassland, especially in the Mississippi Valley
13. A horse-drawn coach that carried passengers, parcels, and mail on scheduled trips over a regular route
14. An apparatus that converts a coded message into electric impulses and sends it to a distant receiver
15. Something that crosses a continent